Terrific
TRAINS

KT-494-957

For Mandy, John, Chloe and Charlie – T.M.
For Gorran – A.P.

KINGFISHER
An imprint of Kingfisher Publications Plc
New Penderel House, 283-288 High Holborn
London WC1V 7HZ

First published in hardback by Kingfisher 1998
First published in paperback by Kingfisher 2000
2 4 6 8 10 9 7 5 3 1

1TR/0999/TWP/RPR(FR)/AMA170

Text copyright © Tony Mitton 1998
Illustrations copyright © Ant Parker 1998

The moral right of the author and illustrator has been asserted. All rights reserved.
No part of this publication may be reproduced, stored in a retrieval system or transmitted
by any means, electronic, mechanical, photocopying or otherwise, without the prior
permission of the publisher.

A CIP catalogue record for this book is available from the British Library.

ISBN 0 7534 0349 8

Printed in Singapore

Terrific
TRAINS

Tony Mitton
and
Ant Parker

KINGFISHER

Big trains, small trains, old trains and new,

rattling and whistling – choo, choo, choo!

Starting from the station with a whistle and a hiss,

steam trains puffing and chuffing like this.

Diesel trains rushing as they rattle down the line,

warning us they're coming with a long, low whine.

Metal wheels whirl as they whizz along the track.
They shimmer and they swish
with a slick click-clack.

Carriages are coupled in a neat, long chain.
An engine pulls the carriages,
and that makes a train.

If a train meets a river or a valley or a ridge,

the train goes over on a big, strong bridge.

If a train meets a mountain it doesn't have to stop

It travels through a tunnel and your ears go pop!

When too many trains try to share the same track.

the signals and the points have to hold some back.

When the rail meets a road,
there's a crossing with a gate.

The train rushes through
while the traffic has to wait.

Trains travel anytime, even very late.

This train's delivering a big load of freight.

This train's for passengers.
We'll soon be on our way.

All aboard and wave goodbye –
we're off on holiday!

Train bits

rails

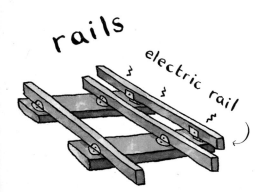

electric rail

these are metal strips that form a pathway called a **track** or **railway line** – some trains get their power from an electric rail

whistle

this makes a noise to warn everyone that the train is coming

wagon

this is for carrying goods, called **freight**

signal

this tells train drivers when to stop and go

carriage

this is for carrying people, called **passengers**

Points

these are rails that move to let the railway line divide so the train changes direction